WRITING NUMBERS IN WORD FORMAT 1 - 50

MATH 1ST GRADE

Children's Math Books

Counting numbers is fun, you also have to know how to write them out in words too!

Are you ready to count and write?

This workbook will help you get familiar with each number and practice your writing.

Have fun writing!

Numbers 1-50

1	2	3	4	5
6	7	8	9	10
11	12	13	14	15
16	17	18	19	20
21	22	23	24	25
26	27	28	29	30
31	32	33	34	35
36	37	38	39	40
41	42	43	44	45
46	47	48	49	50

Writing numbers 1 - 10

You have to learn and remember well how to write the numbers
from
1 to 10 in English.

0

Zero

Zero   Zero

Zero   Zero

Zero   Zero

Zero   Zero

Zero   Zero

Zero   Zero

1

One One
One One
One One
One One
One One
One One

2

Two

Two   Two

Two   Two

Two   Two

Two   Two

Two   Two

3

Three

Three   Three

Three   Three

Three   Three

Three   Three

Three   Three

Three   Three

4

Four

Four   Four

Four   Four

Four   Four

Four   Four

Four   Four

5

Five Five

Five Five

Five Five

Five Five

Five Five

Five Five

6

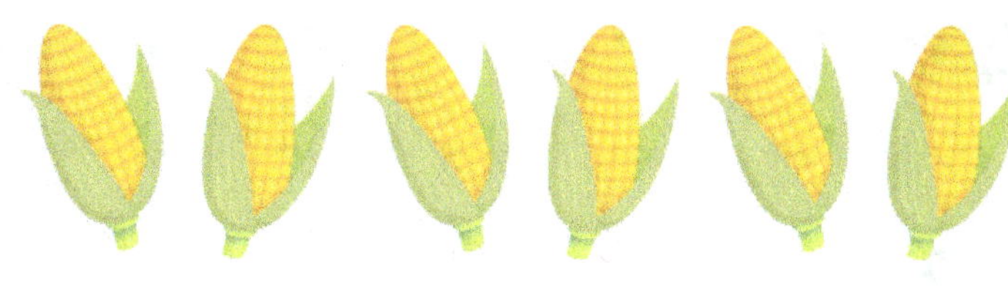

Six Six

Six Six

Six Six

Six Six

Six Six

Six Six

7

Seven Seven
Seven Seven
Seven Seven
Seven Seven
Seven Seven
Seven Seven

8

Eight

Eight Eight
Eight Eight
Eight Eight
Eight Eight
Eight Eight
Eight Eight

9

Nine

Nine

Nine

Nine

Nine

Nine

Nine

Nine

Nine

Nine

Nine

10

Ten

Ten

Ten

Ten

Ten

Ten

Ten

Ten

Ten

Ten

Ten

Writing numbers 11-20

Numbers **11** to **20** have a particular name that you need to know and are also spelled in a different way. This is how you write them.

11

Eleven

Eleven

Eleven Eleven

Eleven Eleven

Eleven Eleven

Eleven Eleven

Eleven Eleven

12

Twelve

Twelve   Twelve

Twelve   Twelve

Twelve   Twelve

Twelve   Twelve

Twelve   Twelve

13

Thirteen

Thirteen   Thirteen

Thirteen   Thirteen

Thirteen   Thirteen

Thirteen   Thirteen

Thirteen   Thirteen

14

Fourteen

Fourteen Fourteen

Fourteen Fourteen

Fourteen Fourteen

Fourteen Fourteen

Fourteen Fourteen

15

Fifteen

Fifteen   Fifteen

Fifteen   Fifteen

Fifteen   Fifteen

Fifteen   Fifteen

Fifteen   Fifteen

16

Sixteen

Sixteen

Sixteen

Sixteen

Sixteen

Sixteen

Sixteen

Sixteen

Sixteen

Sixteen

Sixteen

Sixteen

17

Seventeen Seventeen

Seventeen Seventeen

Seventeen Seventeen

Seventeen Seventeen

Seventeen Seventeen

Seventeen Seventeen

18

Eighteen

Eighteen Eighteen

Eighteen Eighteen

Eighteen Eighteen

Eighteen Eighteen

Eighteen Eighteen

19

Nineteen

Nineteen

Nineteen   Nineteen

Nineteen   Nineteen

Nineteen   Nineteen

Nineteen   Nineteen

Nineteen   Nineteen

20

Twenty

Twenty

Twenty Twenty

Twenty Twenty

Twenty Twenty

Twenty Twenty

Twenty Twenty

Writing numbers 21-30

The numbers after 20 are now quite easy to remember.

21

Twenty-one

Twenty-one Twenty-one

Twenty-one

Twenty-one

Twenty-one

Twenty-one

Twenty-one

22

Twenty-two Twenty-two

Twenty-two

Twenty-two

Twenty-two

Twenty-two

Twenty-two

23

Twenty-three

Twenty-three

Twenty-three

Twenty-three

Twenty-three

Twenty-three

24

Twenty-four

Twenty-four

Twenty-four

Twenty-four

Twenty-four

Twenty-four

25

Twenty-five Twenty-five

Twenty-five

Twenty-five

Twenty-five

Twenty-five

Twenty-five

26

Twenty-six Twenty-six

Twenty-six

Twenty-six

Twenty-six

Twenty-six

Twenty-six

27

Twenty-seven

Twenty-seven

Twenty-seven

Twenty-seven

Twenty-seven

Twenty-seven

28

Twenty-eight

Twenty-eight

Twenty-eight

Twenty-eight

Twenty-eight

Twenty-eight

29

Twenty-nine

Twenty-nine

Twenty-nine

Twenty-nine

Twenty-nine

Twenty-nine

30

Thirty

Thirty   Thirty

Thirty   Thirty

Thirty   Thirty

Thirty   Thirty

Thirty   Thirty

Writing numbers 31-50

These numbers are easy to remember.

31

Thirty-one Thirty-one

Thirty-one

Thirty-one

Thirty-one

Thirty-one

Thirty-one

32

Thirty-two Thirty-two

Thirty-two

Thirty-two

Thirty-two

Thirty-two

Thirty-two

Thirty-three

Thirty-three

Thirty-three

Thirty-three

Thirty-three

Thirty-three

Thirty-three

34

Thirty-four

Thirty-four
Thirty-four
Thirty-four
Thirty-four
Thirty-four
Thirty-four

35

Thirty-five Thirty-five

Thirty-five

Thirty-five

Thirty-five

Thirty-five

Thirty-five

36

Thirty-six   Thirty-six

Thirty-six

Thirty-six

Thirty-six

Thirty-six

Thirty-six

37

Thirty-seven

Thirty-seven

Thirty-seven

Thirty-seven

Thirty-seven

Thirty-seven

38

Thirty-eight Thirty-eight

Thirty-eight

Thirty-eight

Thirty-eight

Thirty-eight

Thirty-eight

39

Thirty-nine Thirty-nine

Thirty-nine

Thirty-nine

Thirty-nine

Thirty-nine

Thirty-nine

40

Forty

Forty

Forty

Forty

Forty

Forty

Forty

Forty

39

Thirty-nine Thirty-nine

Thirty-nine

Thirty-nine

Thirty-nine

Thirty-nine

Thirty-nine

40

Forty

Forty

Forty

Forty

Forty

Forty

Forty

41

Forty-one Forty-one

Forty-one

Forty-one

Forty-one

Forty-one

Forty-one

42

Forty-two Forty-two

Forty-two

Forty-two

Forty-two

Forty-two

Forty-two

43

Forty-three Forty-three

Forty-three

Forty-three

Forty-three

Forty-three

Forty-three

44

Forty-four Forty-four

Forty-four

Forty-four

Forty-four

Forty-four

Forty-four

43

Forty-three Forty-three

Forty-three

Forty-three

Forty-three

Forty-three

Forty-three

44

Forty-four Forty-four

Forty-four

Forty-four

Forty-four

Forty-four

Forty-four

45

Forty-five Forty-five

Forty-five

Forty-five

Forty-five

Forty-five

Forty-five

46

Forty-six Forty-six

Forty-six

Forty-six

Forty-six

Forty-six

Forty-six

47

Forty-seven Forty-seven

Forty-seven

Forty-seven

Forty-seven

Forty-seven

Forty-seven

48

Forty-eight Forty-eight

Forty-eight

Forty-eight

Forty-eight

Forty-eight

Forty-eight

49

Forty-nine Forty-nine

Forty-nine

Forty-nine

Forty-nine

Forty-nine

Forty-nine

50

Fifty

Great Job!

Visit
BABY PROFESSOR
EDUCATION KIDS
www.BabyProfessorBooks.com
to download Free Baby Professor eBooks and view
our catalog of new and exciting Children's Books